comix

THE GOOSE WHO KNEW TOO MUCH

Peter Utton

A & C Black • London

comix

1 **Joker** · Anthony Masters
2 **Sam's Dream** · Michael Hardcastle
3 **Arf and the Greedy Grabber** · Philip Wooderson
4 **Jack's Tree** · Georgia Byng
5 **The Planet Machine** · Steve Bowkett
6 **Mr Potts the Potty Teacher** · Colin West
7 **Henry's Magic Powers** · Peter Utton
8 **Yikes, it's a Yeti!** · Karen Wallace
9 **Arf and the Metal Detector** · Philip Wooderson
10 **Uncle Tom's Pterodactyl** · Colin West
11 **Please Don't Eat my Sister!** · Caroline Pitcher
12 **Monster School** · Garry Kilworth
13 **Hot Air** · Anthony Masters
14 **A Ghost Behind the Stars** · Chris Powling
15 **The Goose Who Knew Too Much** · Peter Utton
16 **Freddy's Fox** · Anthony Masters
17 **Archie's Amazing Game** · Michael Hardcastle
18 **Arf and the Three Dogs** · Philip Wooderson

Published 2002 by A & C Black Publishers Ltd
37 Soho Square, London W1D 3QZ
www.acblack.com

ISBN 0-7136-6176-3

A CIP catalogue record for this book is available from the
British Library.

A & C Black uses paper produced with elemental, chlorine-free pulp,
harvested from managed sustainable forests.

Printed and bound in Spain by G. Z. Printek, Bilbao

CHAPTER ONE

A wandering goose heard the sound of voices...

Myrna, Stuart and Robert were having a picnic with their dog Trixie.
What did you make them with – pebble dust?

Perhaps they are a bit overdone...

I suppose we could use it as a cricket ball...

Yeah? Well catch this then!

The goose was hungry...

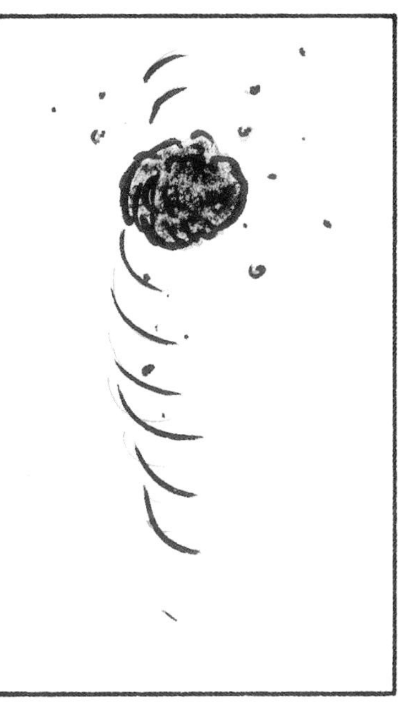

'ONK!

Is it dead?
It was only a cake, Stuart – not a rock!
He's waking up.
There's an address tag.

Pond Cottage, Mill Lane, Hopston. I think I know where that is. It's not far.
He looks a bit groggy. You'd better carry him, Stuart.

Why me?
Careful. Don't scare him...

They all set off...

...unaware that they were being watched.

We forgot to bring the cakes.
Oh dear!
How sad, never mind!

Oi! You lot!

Myrna, Stuart and Robert pulled up fast.

A likely story!
Give it here!

There, there, baby.
What've those horrible
kids been doing to you?

CHAPTER TWO

Well that's nice! That was obviously this year's Mr Charming.
You're quiet, Myrna...
What, you think it's not his?
Why would anyone want to steal a duck – I mean, goose?
Perhaps it lays golden eggs!
Maybe he wants to cook its goose!

Look you two, stop
being stupid. I'm worried
about that goose. Think
of something useful...
We could
check it
out. We've
still got the
address!
Later...
That must be it.
Pond Cottage...

Suddenly an upstairs window burst open...

Er, no, it's only us. We've come to see if the goose is okay.

Goose? You've seen Galahad? Wait. Wait there. I'll be down!

Hello! Please come in. You've seen Galahad? You've seen the goose?

You mean he isn't here?
But we gave it to a man who said it was his...

Really? Was it a blind man with a stick who looked exactly like me?
No, nothing like you. He had black hair and orange sidewhiskers.
And he wasn't too charming either!

The man looked anxious and he paced around the room.
Oh dear! That sounds like Mr Stalecrust. A rather nasty piece of work from the town. He's been trying to buy Galahad for some time now.

Galahad belongs to my twin brother, Jed, and now Jed's gone missing, and he's blind... and...

...and I'm forgetting my manners. I'm Joe and would you like some refreshment? Er, milk? Something fizzy? A banana? Piece of cake?

Joe began to tell his story.
Jed won't sell Galahad even though the pond has dried up. Galahad loved splashing about in it.
Jed went for a stroll this morning but he hasn't returned. Galahad must have gone looking for him.
Lovely cake this, Joe, not a bit hard...
Or rock-like!

Joe looked uneasy...

Well, the strange fact is, Galahad, the goose, is a bit psychic! You know what psychic means?

Yep.
Absolutely!
Mmm...

It means he can see the future – well – a bit of the future... Are you following me?
Absolutely!
Yep.
Mmm...

The amazing thing is, Galahad somehow knows who the winners will be at the local horse races! And the only person who understands what Galahad says is my brother Jed!

Myrna, let's get out of here! He's flipped... loopy... lost his marbles... barmy!

And somehow that rogue Mr Stalecrust has got to hear of our little secret...
And thinks he can force Jed and the goose to give him the names of the winners.
Then he can bet on it and make himself loads of dosh!
Oh poor Jed. Poor Galahad!

Stuart was not taking Joe, or his story, very seriously.
Yes, it's a tragic story, but we ought to be getting along.
No we ought NOT, Stuart! The least we can do is help!

Help? What can we do?
We could watch the betting shop to see if old Stalecrust puts a bet on.
Good grief, Robert, that's a GOOD IDEA!
You wait here, Joe, and we'll report back to you.
Right you are, Myrna, and thank you so much!

You're not serious, Myrna. He's obviously barking mad!
I don't think he is. And his brother and Galahad are missing...
That's if he's got a blind twin brother!

CHAPTER THREE
Two days later...
ERNIE'S BETTING SHOP
Myrna, this is so boring. Old Stalecrust is not going to...
Wait! Look.
There he is. He's going in...
Half an hour later...
What's he doing in there. He's been hours!
He's put a bet on, and he's waiting to see if he's won.

The door's opening... it's him!
He doesn't look too happy...
Definitely UNHAPPY, I'd say!
Grrr!
His horse must have come last!
Let's follow him. He might lead us to Jed and the goose.

CHAPTER FOUR

You idiot, Stuart! It's Jed who's been telling Stalecrust the wrong horses.
But that would make Mr Stalecrust even angrier. And then what will he do to Jed and Galahad!
Mmm...
I've got a cunning plan. If Joe is Jed's twin brother...

...we could dress him up to look like Jed. Give him a stick and dark glasses.
What's the point of that, genius?

Then old Stalecrust sees him around town, and thinks Jed has escaped!

And then Stalecrust rushes back to where he's hiding them...

...and we follow him and he leads us to Jed and Galahad!

I don't believe it...

...but that is a brilliant idea!

CHAPTER FIVE

Joe found a spare pair of dark glasses, a white stick and one of Jed's berets.

Joe flung open the door.
What a lark eh, heroes! Let's go!
Wait, Joe. Hang on a minute!
Joe, you can't just go charging in like a... a...

Like a rock cake on fire?
For the plan to work we have to be very careful and very clever.
Message understood, skipper!
We have to convince Stalecrust that you are your brother.

CHAPTER SIX

The very next day they saw the villain leaving the betting shop.

No, Joe, wait. We must stick to the plan!

Look, he's gone into a pub.
No doubt to celebrate his winnings!
Some time later Mr Stalecrust staggered from the pub.

He looks a bit wobbly!
The blighter's squiffy! Too much ale!

Now's our chance, Joe.

They followed Mr Stalecrust into the shopping centre.

Right, Stu, give him a blast on the whistle!

HONK!
AHH!

Wassat? Eh? Sounded like a goo...

No, couldn't be. Urgh! Who's that? Looks like...

Mr Stalecrust peered into a shop, but jumped as he saw the reflection of a familiar figure.

It's him! The blind fella. But how?

HONK!
ARGH!

Wh-wherzat goo-goose?

Am I going crazy? Or...

Perhaps they've escaped!
Nah, that's impossible!

Better check to be sure!
Yes! He's fallen for it. Quick let's follow him!

He's leaving town...

He can't be going too far on foot.

He seems to be heading for your place, Joe!

No, he's turned off.
I wonder...

Joe jumped up and rushed down the hill.
Come on. I think I know where he's going.
Of course. The old water mill!
Wait till he goes in, Joe.
Look. He's dammed the stream!

The crafty blighter.
That's why Galahad's
pond dried up!
In the mill a confused Mr Stalecrust was
checking a small, locked room.
Now to see if
they've escaped!
So you are
still here!
HSSSS!
HSSSS!

Of course we're still here, you fiend! Do you think we've been out for an afternoon stroll?

Well, what's going on then? I saw... in town... I heard...

There's something fishy going on...
Talking of fish. Galahad and I haven't eaten anything since yesterday...

Tough! I'm going to sort this out.

The gang of five rushed into the mill.

We're here, Jed! We're here!
HONK!
HONK!
HONK!
HONK!
Jed, I want you to meet some friends of mine.

One girl, two boys, and a little four footed hero, if I'm not mistaken! I feel I know you already!
Like two peas in a pod!
And twice as potty!
We'll undam the stream before we go, and then Galahad can have his pond back!
Brilliant, my gallant gang!

Everyone dived behind the bushes –
except Joe...

The sun glittering, the birds twittering, eh what?
Never mind the birds twittering!
Let's get you back inside!
One moment, my dear old crust...
I believe we owe you this!
Ooof!

Oooh! How d'yer know where I was?

It's a puzzle, isn't it, my old rascal. Perhaps it was a fluke...

THWACK!
Let's try again. Oops!

OW! You're a proper devil and no mistake!
Here, how come you've had a shave? And you've changed your pullover!
It's the goose, you know. He's not only a fortune teller. He's a wizard as well!
He can also turn himself into a ferocious crust-eater!

Meanwhile, round the side of the mill, Rob and Stu had nearly undammed the stream.

The stream was undammed and water rushed through...

...and hit the mill wheel.

Galahad and Trixie were a fierce team.

SPLADOOMPH!

Uggh!

Woooh!

SPLADUNK!
OGGLE! UGGLE!

Hello, hello. What's going on here then?

Sergeant Willis. A lovely morning. What brings you out here?
Help!

When I suddenly heard a strange honking noise in my head...

And if I'm not mistaken, that looks like a rather soggy Stalecrust.
One almost feels sorry for the old rascal...
SPLUNCH!
Yes... almost...
I'd better hear the whole story.
Urgh... Help!
Well, it all started the other day. I'd made some delicious little cakes for a picnic...
Helbub!
Delicious cakes... yes... not so fast, young lady.

CHAPTER SEVEN
Well, well, Jack, up to your old tricks again?
I'll confess to everything... anything! Just get me out of here!
We could say, you're coming 'clean', eh Jack? Ha, Ha!
They're all mad! Bonkers!
That goose isn't a real goose, sergeant. It's a wizard.
Of course it is, Jack.

Then they all traipsed back to the cottage.
Well, young heroes, how can we ever thank you?
Absolutely, eh, what?

Wait, Galahad has a message for you. It's a sure winner in tomorrow's race!

Er, no thanks very much! We're not betting people.
Eh? Now hang on!

Bye, then. Thanks again. See you soon.

Myrna, we could've made our fortune with Galahad's winner!
Changed your mind about the magic duck then, Stuart?
Certainly not! Anyway it's not a magic duck... it's a magic goose!